Guess What!

Student's Book 1

American English

Susannah Reed with Kay Bentley

Series Editor: Lesley Koustaff

CAMBRIDGE
UNIVERSITY PRESS

Contents

Hello!

Guess What!

1 CD1 03 Listen. Who's speaking?

2 CD1 04 Listen, point, and say.

3 CD1 05 Listen and find.

Find Leo

4 CD1 06 **Say the chant.**

5 Think **Look and say the name.**

Number 1. David.

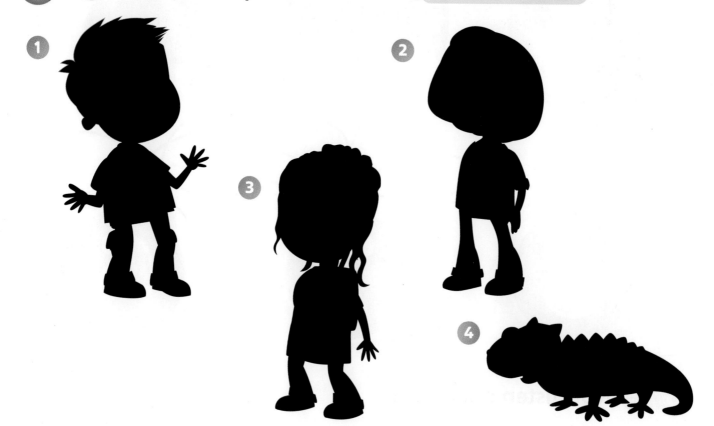

1

2

3

4

6 CD1 09 **Listen, look, and say.**

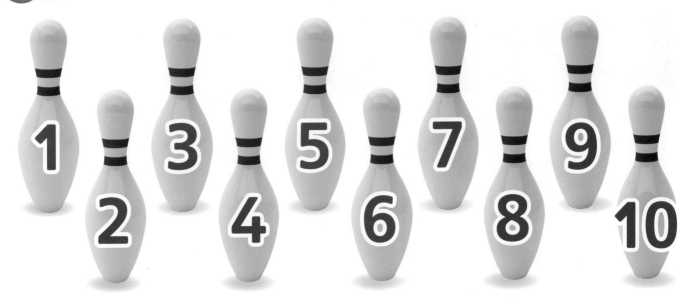

1 2 3 4 5 6 7 8 9 10

7 **Look and match.**

1
2
3

8
7
6

8 CD1 10 **Now listen and check.**

9 CD1 12 **Listen, point, and say.**

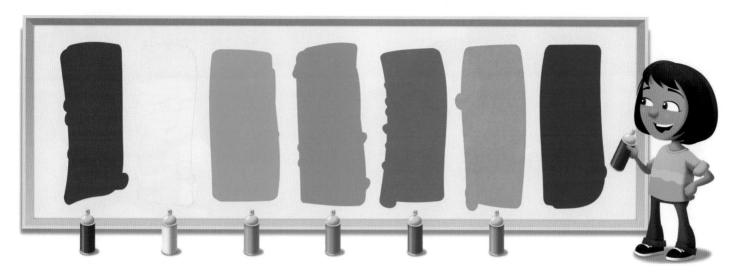

10 CD1 13 **Sing the song.**

11 About Me **Ask and answer.**

How old are you?   I'm six.

What's your favorite color?   My favorite color's blue.

12 CD1 15 **Listen.**

10 Value: Be curious

→ Workbook page 8

13   **Listen and act.**

Animal sounds

14 (CD1 18) **Listen and say.**

A **p**ink and **p**urple **p**anda.

What **color** is it?

1 CD1 20 Listen and say.

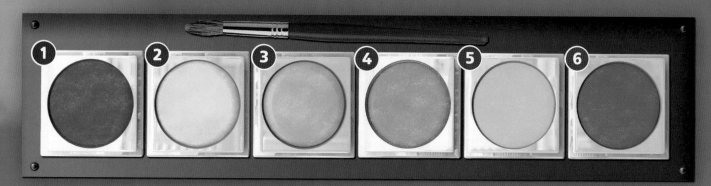

2 Watch the video.

3 Say the color.

Number 1. Orange. Yes.

Guess What!

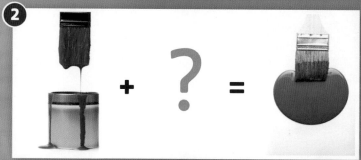

Project

4 Make a rainbow.

1 School

Guess What!

15

1 (CD1 22) Listen. Who's speaking?

2 (CD1 23) Listen, point, and say.

3 (CD1 24) Listen and find.

Find Leo

16 Vocabulary → Workbook page 12

4 (CD1 26) Say the chant.

5 (Think) Look and find five differences.

Picture 1. A purple pen.   Picture 2. A purple pencil.

6 (CD1 28) **Sing the song.**

7 (CD1 29) **Listen and answer the questions.**

How many chairs can you see?

Six!

8 CD1 30 **Listen, point, and say.**

9 CD1 31 **Listen and do the action.**

10 **Play the game.**

Open your book.

Grammar: *Stand up, please.* **19**

12 **Talk Time** Listen and act.

Animal sounds

13 CD1 36 Listen and say.

A **bear** with a **blue** book.

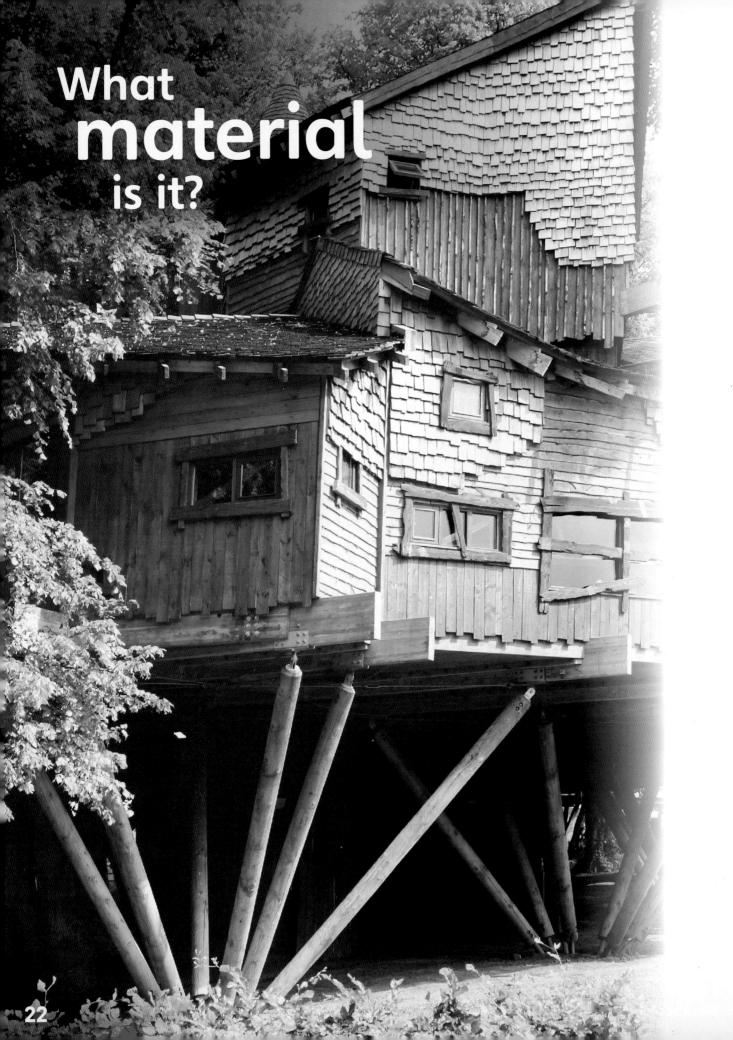

What
material
is it?

1 CD1 38 **Listen and say.**

2 **Watch the video.**

3 **Look and say *wood*, *plastic*, *metal*, or *glass*.**

Number 1. Wood.   Yes.

Guess What!

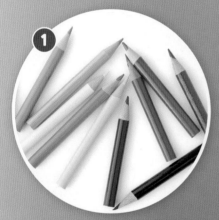

Project

4 **Draw materials in your classroom.**

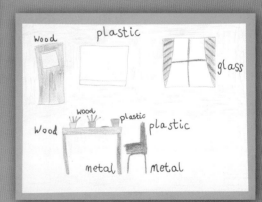

CLIL: Science   **23**

Guess What!

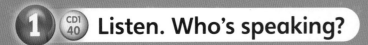

1 (CD1 40) **Listen. Who's speaking?**

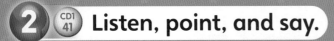

2 (CD1 41) **Listen, point, and say.**

3 (CD1 42) **Listen and find.**

Find Leo

Say the chant.

5 **Look and find five missing toys in picture 2.**

The yellow ball.

→ Workbook page 21

6 CD1 46 **Listen, look, and say.**

7 Think **Look and say.** What's this? It's a kite.

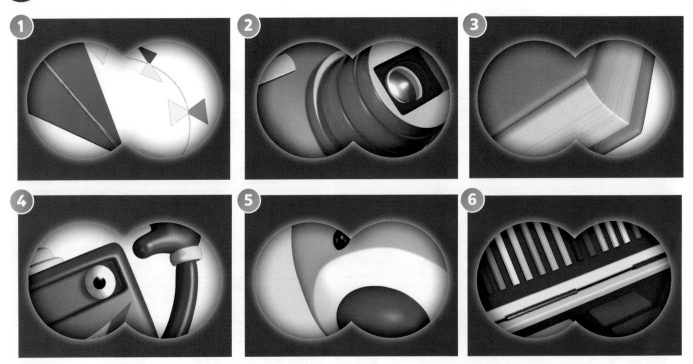

8 CD1 47 **Now listen and check.**

9 (CD1 49) **Sing the song.**

10 Play the game.

Is it a ball?

No, it isn't.

Value: Say thank you

→ Workbook page 24

12 **CD1 54** **Talk Time** **Listen and act.**

Animal sounds

13 **CD1 55** **Listen and say.**

A turtle with two teddy bears.

Is it
electric?

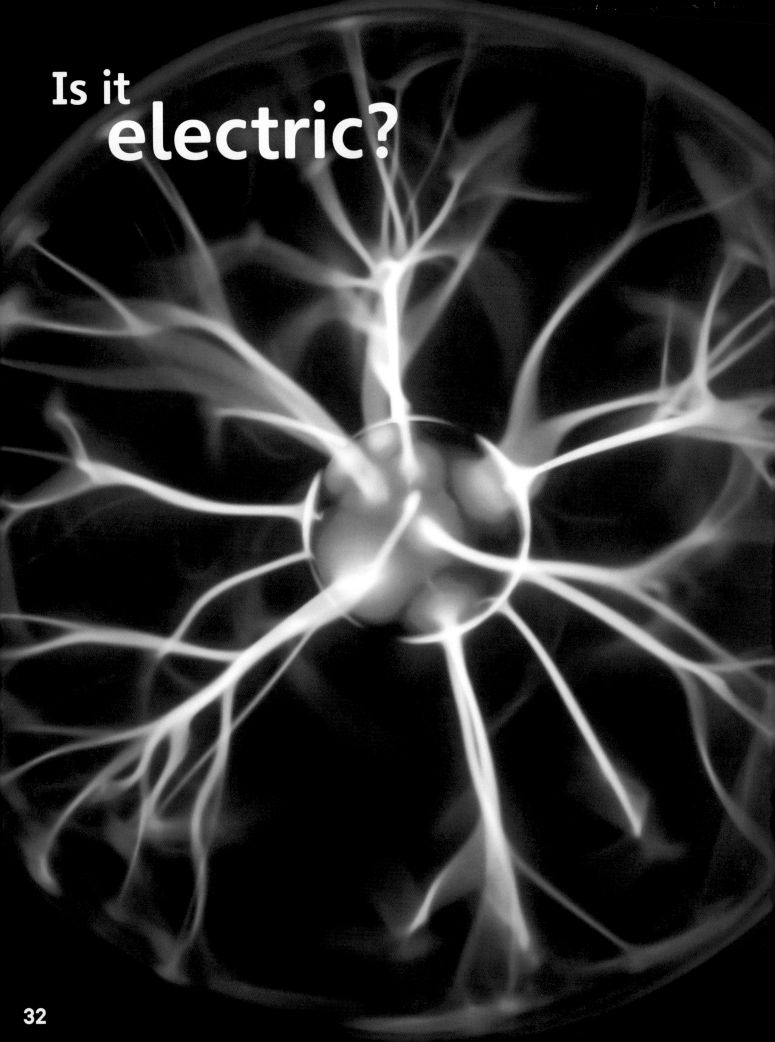

1 🔊 CD1 57 **Listen and say.**

1

2

3

2 **Watch the video.**

3 **Look and say *it's electric*, or *it isn't electric*.**

Number 1. It isn't electric. Yes.

Guess What!

1

2

Project

4 **Draw an electric toy.**

3

4

→ Workbook page 26

Review Units 1 and 2

1 Look and say the word. Number 1. Desk.

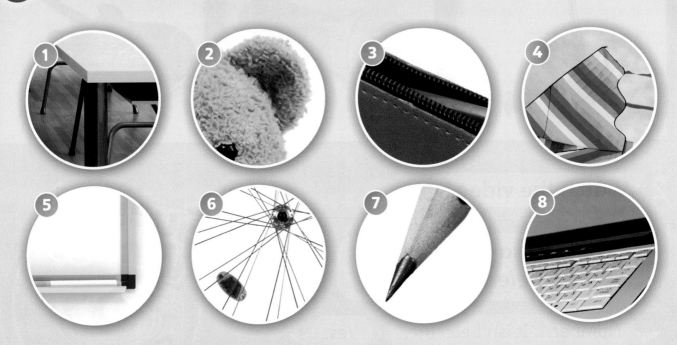

2 CD1 59 Listen and say the color.

→ Workbook pages 28–29

Blue
What's this?
It's a (pencil case).

Red
Is it a (teddy bear)?
Yes, it is.
Is it an (art set)?
No, it isn't.

Finish

12

10

11

9

8

6

7

5

4

3

Yellow
How many books can you see?
I can see (six books).

1

2

Start

35

③ Family

Guess What!

1 (CD2 02) **Listen. Who's speaking?**

2 (CD2 03) **Listen, point, and say.**

 grandma

2 grandpa

3 dad **4** mom **5** uncle **6** aunt

7 brother **8** sister **9** cousin

3 (CD2 04) **Listen and find.**

Find Leo

4 CD2 05 **Say the chant.**

5 CD2 06 Think **Listen and say *yes* or *no*.** This is my dad. No!

6 CD2 08 **Sing the song.**

7 CD2 09 Think **Listen and say *yes* or *no*.**

8 CD2 10 **Listen, look, and say.**

9 CD2 11 **Listen and say the color.**

10 About Me **Draw your family. Ask and answer.**

Who's this?　It's my brother. His name's Freddy.

Who's that? Is that your sister?　No, it isn't. It's my cousin.

Value: Love your family

→ Workbook page 34

12   **Listen and act.**

Animal sounds

13 **Listen and say.**

A **d**olphin in a re**d** **d**esk.

What
continent
is it?

Ottawa

Madrid

Tokyo

Lima

1 (CD2 18) **Listen and say.**

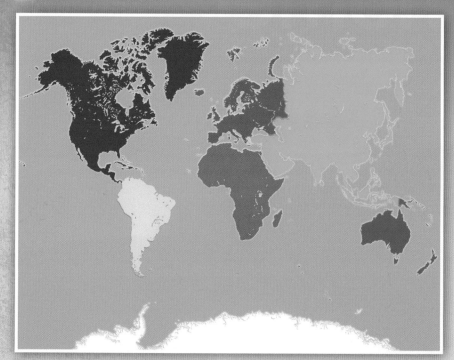

1 North America
2 South America
3 Europe
4 Africa
5 Asia
6 Australia
7 Antarctica

2 **Watch the video.**

3 **What continent are they from?**

My name's Akio. I'm from Tokyo.

My name's Zack. I'm from Ottawa.

My name's Luiz. I'm from Lima.

My name's Sofia. I'm from Madrid.

Project

4 **Color and stick the continents.**

CLIL: Geography **45**

4 At home

Guess What!

1 CD2 21 **Listen. Who's speaking?**

2 CD2 22 **Listen, point, and say.**

① house
② bathroom
③ bedroom
④ apartment
⑤ dining room
⑥ living room
⑦ balcony
⑧ kitchen
⑨ hallway
⑩ yard

Find Leo

3 CD2 23 **Listen and find.**

4 CD2 24 **Say the chant.**

5 Think **Look and say the room.**

Number 1. Dining room.

6 CD2 26 Listen, look, and say.

1

2

3

7 CD2 27 Listen and say Apartment 1 or Apartment 2.

Where's your Mom?

Apartment 2.

She's in the bedroom.

Apartment 1

Apartment 2

8 (CD2 28) **Sing the song.**

9 (CD2 29) **Listen and say *yes* or *no*.**

10 **Ask and answer.**

Where's the doll?

It's under the table.

Yes!

Grammar: *Where's the doll?* **51**

Value: Take care of things

→ Workbook page 42

12 **Talk Time** **Listen and act.**

Animal sounds

13 **Listen and say.**

An ant with an apple.

What shape is it?

1 (CD2 36) **Listen and say.**

circle

triangle

square

2 **Watch the video.**

3 **Look and say** *circle*, *triangle*, **or** *square*.

What's this?   It's a circle!

Guess What!

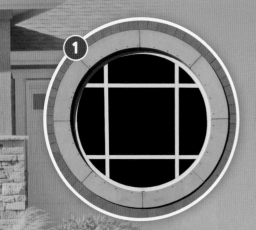

Project

4 Make a shapes picture.

Review Units 3 and 4

1 Look and say the words. Number 1. Yard.

2 CD2 37 Listen and say the color.

→ Workbook pages 46–47

Yellow
Where's the (computer)?
It's (in) the (bedroom).

Orange
Where's your (grandma)?
(She) is in the (bedroom).

Start

Finish

5 My body

Guess What!

1 CD2 38 Listen. Who's speaking?

2 CD2 39 Listen, point, and say.

1 head

2 nose

3 eyes

4 hair

5 ears

6 arms

7 mouth

8 hands

9 feet

10 legs

BIKE CLUB

Find Leo

3 CD2 40 Listen and find.

4 CD2 41 Say the chant.

5 Think Look and say the action.

Number 1. Stamp your feet.

1

2

3

→ Workbook page 49

6 CD2 43 **Listen, look, and say.**

7 CD2 44 Think **Listen and say the name.**

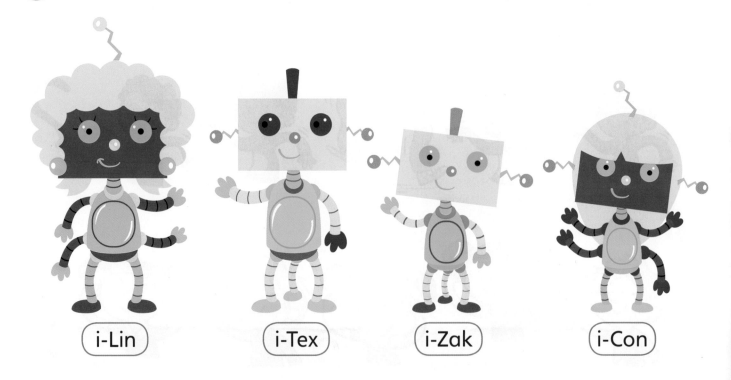

i-Lin   i-Tex   i-Zak   i-Con

8 (CD2 46) **Sing the song.**

9 **Ask and answer.**

Do you have a blue nose and two purple arms?

Yes, I do.

Number 3!

Grammar: *Do you have a yellow nose?* **63**

10 ^{CD2 47} Listen.

Value: Be clean

→ Workbook page 52

11   **Listen and act.**

Animal sounds

12 **Listen and say.**

An iguana with pink ink.

What sense is it?

1 CD2 52 **Listen and say.**

sight

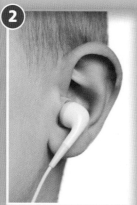
hearing

smell

taste

touch

2 **Watch the video.**

3 **Look and say the senses.**

Number 1. Sight and touch.   Yes.

Guess What!

Project

4 Make a senses poster.

CLIL: Science **67**

6 Food

Guess What!

1 CD3 02 **Listen. Who's speaking?**

2 CD3 03 **Listen, point, and say.**

1 chicken
2 water
3 orange
4 cheese
5 milk
6 egg
7 apple
8 banana
9 juice
10 bread

3 CD3 04 **Listen and find.**

Find Leo

4 CD3 05 **Say the chant.**

5 Think **Look and find five differences.**

Picture 1. I have chicken.   Picture 2. I have cheese.

6 CD3 07 Listen, look, and say.

1

2

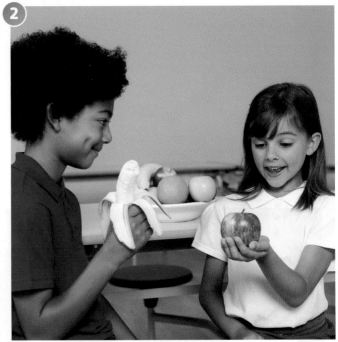

7 CD3 08 Think Listen and say the name.

> I like chicken, and I like bananas ...

> Kim.

		🍗	🍌	🥛	🥛
Alex		✗	✓	✗	✓
Sasha		✓	✗	✓	✗
Sam		✗	✓	✓	✗
Kim		✓	✓	✓	✗

8 CD3 10 **Sing the song.**

9 About Me **Play the game.**

Number 1. Yellow. Do you like chicken with apples?   No, I don't.

Grammar: *Do you like eggs?* **73**

74 Value: Be patient

→ Workbook page 60

Talk Time **Listen and act.**

CD3 13

Animal sounds

12 CD3 14 **Listen and say.**

An elephant with ten eggs.

Where is **food** from?

1 CD3 16 Listen and say.

plants

animals

2 Watch the video.

3 Look and say *plant* or *animal*.

Number 1. Plant. Yes!

Guess What!

Project

4 Make a food and drink poster.

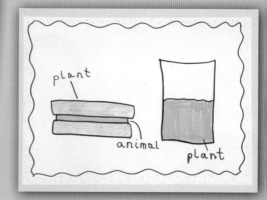

Review Units 5 and 6

1 Look and say the word.

> Number 1. Mouth.

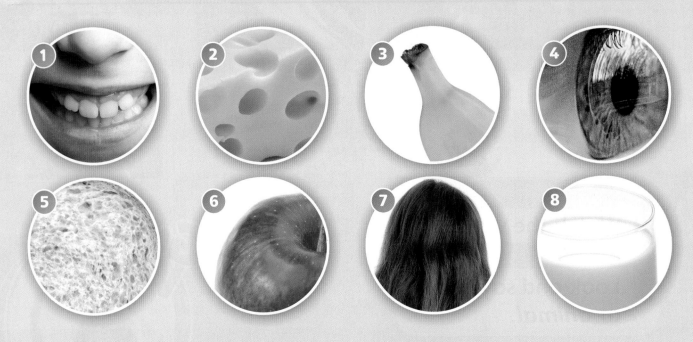

2 CD3 17 Listen and say the name.

Tony

Ana

Lily

Ravi

→ Workbook pages 64–65

3 Play the game.

Finish

Start

Blue
I don't have (four hands).
I have a (nose).

Green
I like / I don't like
(bananas).

(7) Actions

Guess What!

Come to a **Festival** at the park!

1. run
2. jump
3. swim
4. climb
5. play soccer
6. ride a bike
7. draw
8. paint
9. dance
10. sing

3 CD3 20 **Listen and find.**

Find Leo

4 CD3 21 **Say the chant.**

5 **Look and match. Then say the action.**

Number 1. Green.
Play soccer.

1  **2**  **3**  **4**

→ Workbook page 67

6 CD3 23 **Listen, look, and say.**

1

2

7 CD3 24 **Listen and say the number.** I can run. Six.

1

2

3

4

5

6

8 CD3 26 **Sing the song.**

9 About Me **Ask and answer.**

Can you ride a bike?

Yes, I can.

→ Workbook page 69

Grammar: *Can you ride a bike?* **85**

Value: Help your friends

→ Workbook page 70

11 Listen and act.

Animal sounds

12 Listen and say.

An umbrella
bird can jump.

What's the number?

1 CD3 32 **Listen and say.**

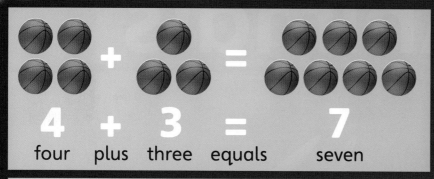

4 + 3 = 7
four plus three equals seven

8 − 2 = 6
eight minus two equals six

Guess What!

2 **Watch the video.**

3 **Find the number. Then say the words.**

Five balls plus five balls equals ten balls. Yes!

①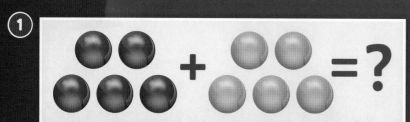

②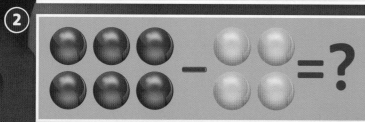

③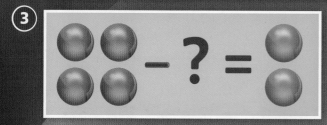

Project

4 Draw two picture sums.

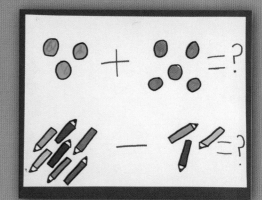

8 Animals

Guess
What!

1 (CD3 33) Listen. Who's speaking?

2 (CD3 34) Listen, point, and say.

1 giraffe

2 monkey

3 elephant　　4 bird

5 snake　　6 hippo

7 zebra

Africa

8 lion

9 spider

10 crocodile

Find Leo

3 (CD3 35) Listen and find.

4 **Say the chant.**

5 (Think) **Look and say the animal.** Number 1. A snake.

 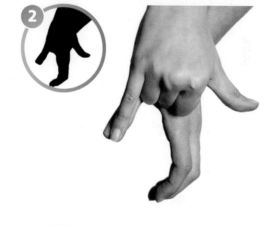

6 CD3 38 Listen, point, and say.

long   short

big   small

tall   short

7 CD3 39 Listen and say the number.

1

2

3

8 CD3 40 **Sing the song.**

9 CD3 41 **Listen and say *yes* or *no*.**

10 **Look and find five mistakes.**

> Giraffes don't have short necks.
> Giraffes have long necks.

12   **Listen and act.**

Animal sounds

13 CD3 45 **Listen and say.**

An octopus in an orange box.

→ Workbook page 79   Functional language: *It's small. Respect animals.* **Pronunciation:** *o* **97**

How do animals move?

1 CD3 47 Listen and say.

①

walk

②

fly

③

slither

2 Watch the video.

3 Look and say *walk*, *fly*, or *slither*.

A spider can walk.   Yes.

①

②

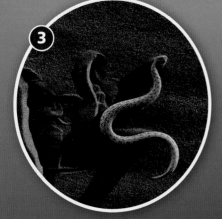

③

④

Guess What!

Project

4 Make an animal movement chart.

Review Units 7 and 8

 Look and say the words.

> Number 1.
> Play soccer.

2 CD3 48 Listen and say the number.

3 Play the game.

Orange
I can (play soccer).

Green
(Giraffes) have (long necks).

Red
(Birds) are (small).

My sounds

panda

bear

turtle

dolphin

ant

iguana

elephant

umbrella bird

octopus

Thanks and Acknowledgments

Many thanks to everyone in the excellent team at Cambridge University Press. In particular we would like to thank Emily Hird, Liane Grainger, Camilla Agnew, and Flavia Lamborghini whose professionalism, enthusiasm, experience, and talent makes them all such a pleasure to work with.

We would also like to give special thanks to Lesley Koustaff for her unfailing support, expert guidance, good humor, and welcome encouragement throughout the project.

The authors and publishers would like to thank the following contributors:

Blooberry Design: concept design, cover design, book design, page makeup

Emma Szlachta: editing

Lisa Hutchins: freelance editing

Ann Thomson: art direction, picture research

Gareth Boden: commissioned photography

Jon Barlow: commissioned photography

Ian Harker: audio recording

Robert Lee, Dib Dib Dub Studios: song and chant composition

Vince Cross: theme tune composition

James Richardson: arrangement of theme tune

John Marshall Media: audio recording and production

Phaebus: video production

hyphen S.A.: publishing management, American English edition

The authors and publishers acknowledge the following sources of copyright material and are grateful for the permissions granted. Although every effort has been made, it has not always been possible to identify the sources of all the material used, or to trace all copyright holders.

If any omissions are brought to our notice, we will be happy to include the appropriate acknowledgments on reprinting.

The authors and publishers would like to thank the following illustrators:

Bill Bolton: pp 28; Chris Jevons (Bright Agency): pp 18, 50, 62, 84, 95; Joelle Dreidemy (Bright Agency): pp 17, 27, 49, 61, 71; Kirsten Collier (Bright Agency): pp 11, 21, 31, 43, 53, 65, 75, 87, 97, 102, 103; Marcus Cutler (Sylvie Poggio): pp 35, 57, 79, 101; Marek Jagucki: pp 5, 6, 9, 10, 15, 16, 20, 25, 26, 30, 37, 38, 39, 42, 47, 48, 52, 56, 59, 60, 64, 69, 70, 74, 81, 82, 86, 91, 92, 96; Mark Duffin: pp 13, 44; Richard Watson (Bright Agency): pp 41, 50, 84; Woody Fox (Bright Agency): pp 18, 29, 40, 51, 63, 73, 85, 95

The authors and publishers would like to thank the following for permission to reproduce photographs:

p.2–3: holbox/Shutterstock; p.4–5: SAMSUL SAID/Reuters/Corbis; p.6 (CL): Fertnig/Getty Images; p.6 (C): Margot Hartford/Alamy; p.6 (CR): Blend Images/Alamy; p.11 (B/G), p.21 (B/G), p.65 (B/G), p.87 (B/G): SZE FEI WONG/Getty Images; p.11 (T): Mike Kemp/Getty Images; p.12–13 (B/G):plusphoto/Getty Images; p.13 (TC): TongoRo Images/Alamy; p.13 (BL): Leigh Prather/Shutterstock; p.13 (BC): Valery Voennyy/Alamy; p.14–15: Pat Canova/Alamy; p.17 (TL): UltraONEs/Getty Images; p.17 (TC): Kimberly Hosey/Getty Images; p.17 (TR): MiguelMalo/Getty Images; p.17 (CL): Vincent St. Thomas/shutterstock; p.17 (C): Picsfive/Shutterstock; p.17 (CR): Dimitris66/Getty Images; p.22–23: VisitBritain/Pawel Libera/Getty Images; p.23 (T-1): Shutterstock/My Life Graphic; p.23 (T-2): Shutterstock/ Vorobyeva; p.23 (T-3): Jesus Keller/Shutterstock; p.23 (T-4): Foonia/Shutterstock, p.23 (B-1): Shutterstock/ETIENjones; p.23 (B-2): bikeriderlondon/Shutterstock; p.23 (B-3): Jerome Skiba/Getty Images; p.23 (B-4): hayatikayhan/Getty Images; p.24–25: Zhang Chunlei/Xinhua Press/Corbis; p.27 (TL): stable/Shutterstock; p.27 (TC): Chesky/Shutterstock; p.27 (TR): ONOKY-Photononstop/Alamy; p.31 (B/G), p.97 (B/G): Jolanta Wojcicka/Shutterstock; p.32–33: Shutterstock/ Anna Rubak; p.33 (TL): ffolas/Shutterstock; p.33 (TC): Prapann/Shutterstock; p.33 (TR): meKCar/Shutterstock; p.33 (CL): Shutterstock/Sergiy Kuzmin; p.33 (C): Shutterstock/Ociacia; p.33 (BL): Shutterstock/HomeStudio; p.33 (BC): Shutterstock/ Chiyacat; p.34 (1): Shutterstock/archideaphoto; p.34 (2): Shutterstock/Picsfive; p.34 (3): Shutterstock/Ingvar Bjork; p.34 (4): sunsetman/Shutterstock; p.34 (5): Shutterstock/Jojje; p.34 (6): Shutterstock/Lim Yong Hian;

p.34 (7): Shutterstock/ Craig Jewell; p.34 (8): Shutterstock/Sergii Figurnyi; p.34 (CL): SuperStock/Tetra Images; p.34 (CR), p.34 (BL): Alamy/MBI; p.34 (BR): SuperStock/AsiaPix; p.36–37: JACQUES Pierre/hemis.fr/Getty Images; p.39 (TL): Blend Images/Alamy; p.39 (TC): Shotshop GmbH/Alamy; p.39 (TR): Shutterstock/Monkey Business Images; p.45 (TL): Ekkaruk Dongpuyow/Alamy; p.45 (CL): mamahoohooba/Alamy; p.45 (CR): Cultura RM/Alamy; p.45 (BL): Keith Levit/Alamy; p.45 (BC): Rick Gomez/Getty Images; p.46–47: Vaughn Greg/Getty Images; p.49 (TL): Simon Montgomery/ Getty Images; p.49 (TR): Compassionate Eye Foundation/Rob Daly/ OJO Images Ltd/ Getty Images; p.49 (CL): DEA/G. DAGLI ORTI/Getty Images; p.49 (CR): Chuck Schmidt/Getty Images; p.53 (B/G), p.75 (B/G): Tim Jackson/Getty Images; p.53 (T): Radius Images/Alamy; p.54–55: romakoma/Shutterstock, p.55 (1): RDFlemming/ Shutterstock; p.55 (2): Alamy/Andrew Holt; p.55 (3): Shotshop GmbH/Alamy; p.55 (4): Alamy/Ros Drinkwater; p.56 (1): Mark Boulton/Alamy; p.56 (3): Shotshop GmbH/Alamy; p.56 (5): Breadmaker/Shutterstock; p.56 (7): Aardvark/Alamy; p.56 (CL): Alamy/Westend61 GmbH; p.56 (CR): Shutterstock/Flashon Studio; p.56 (BL): MBI/Alamy; p.56 (BR): Alamy/Richard Newton; p.58–59: Frans Lemmens/ Corbis; p.61 (TL): Pavel L Photo and Video/Shutterstock; p.61 (TC girl): Gelpi JM/Shutterstock; p.61 (TC boy): Tetra Images/Alamy; p.61 (TR): annie-claude/ Getty Images; p.66–67: gettyimages/Maria Pavlova; p.67 (T-1): Shutterstock/ Federico Rostagno; p.67 (T-2): Shutterstock/Ilya Andriyanov; p.67 (T-3): Evgeny Bakharev/Shutterstock; p.67 (T-4): acilo/Getty Images; p.67 (T-5): YAY Media AS/ Alamy; p.67 (B-1): Valentia_G/Shutterstock; p.67 (B-2): sbarabu/Shutterstock; p.67 (B-3): foodfolio/Alamy; p.67 (B-4): Liunian/shutterstock; p.68–69: Christian Mueller/Shutterstock; p.71 (TL): Serg Salivon/Shutterstock; p.71 (TR): Sea Wave/ Shutterstock; p.71 (CL): ThomsonD/Shutterstock; p.71 (CR): Chursina Viktorlia/ Shutterstock; p.72 (CL): Viktor1/Shutterstock; P.72 (1): Viktor1/Shutterstock; P.72 (C bananas): Sergio33/Shutterstock; p.72 (C milk): Tarasyuk Igor/Shutterstock; p.72 (CR): Anna Kucherova/Shutterstock; p.72 (Alex): R. Gino Santa Maria/Shutterstock; p.72 (Sasha): Jack Hollingsworth/Getty Images; p.72 (Sam): KidStock/Getty Images; p.72 (Kim): Wavebreakmedia Ltd/Getty Images; p.73 (2): v.s.anandhakrishna/ Shutterstock; p.73 (3): saiko3p/Getty Images; p.73 (4), p.73 (BL): Nattika/ Shutterstock; p.73 (5): Christopher Elwell/Shutterstock; p.73 (water): Betacam- SP/Shutterstock; p.73 (juice): Kitch Bain/Shutterstock; p.73 (apples): Garsya/ Shutterstock; p.73 (BR): aarrows/Shutterstock; p.76–77: R. Fassbind/Shutterstock; p.77 (T-1): Shutterstock/colognephotos; p.77 (T-2): Shutterstock/Denis and Yulia Pogostins; p.77 (T-3): pattyphotoart/Shutterstock; p.77 (T-4): Shutterstock/ lightpoet; p.77 (T-5): Shutterstock/holbox; p.77 (T-6): Zoe mack/Alamy; p.77 (B-1): Julian Rovagnati/Shutterstock; p.77 (B-2): Anna Moskvina/Shutterstock; p.77 (B-3): Shutterstock/ffolas; p.77 (B-4): PeJo/Shutterstock; p.78 (1): Shutterstock/xavier gallego morel; p.78 (2): Shutterstock/Christian Draghici; p.78 (3): Shutterstock/ Svetlana Kuznetsova; p.78 (4): Shutterstock/janinajaak; p.78 (5): Shutterstock/ andersphoto; p.78 (6): ell2550/Shutterstock; p.78 (7): Shutterstock/VaclavHroch; p.78 (8): Shutterstock/Valentyn Volkov; p.80–81: Juniors Bildarchiv BmbH/Alamy; p.83 (1): Shutterstock/irin-k; p.83 (2): Shutterstock/Picsfive; p.83 (3): Shutterstock/ Luminis; p.83 (4): Shutterstock/auremar; p.83 (BL): Shutterstock/Pressmaster; p.83 (BC swim), p.83 (BR): Shutterstock/Monkey Business Images; p.83 (BC paint): Shutterstock/Len44ik; p.88–89: Jose Luis Stephens/Getty Images; p.89 (T): Shutterstock/R-O-M-A; p.89 (C): Shutterstock/silavsale; p.90–91: Villiers Steyn/ Shutterstock; p.93 (TL): Stuart Westmorland/Getty Images; p.93 (TC monkey): Don Mammoser/Shutterstock; p.93 (TC bird): Danita Delimont/Getty Images; p.93 (TR): A.Tofke Cologne Germay/Getty Images; p.94 (TL): Maurizio Biso/Shutterstock; p.94 (TR): Matt Ragen/Shutterstock; p.94 (CL): Volodymyr Burdiak/Shutterstock; p.94 (BL): Lintao Zhang/Getty Images; p.94 (BC): Heiko Kiera/Shutterstock; p.94 (BR): PILAR OLIVARES/Reuters/Corbis; p.97 (T): Erica Shires/Corbis; p.98–99: Joe McDonald/Corbis; p.99 (TL): john michael evan potter/Shutterstock; p.99 (TC): Istvan Kadar Photography/Getty Images; p.99 (TR): Purcell Pictures, Inc./Alamy; p.99 (CL): Petra Wegner/Alamy; p.99 (C): Mmphotos/Getty Images; p.99 (BL): Solvin Zankl/Nature Picture Library/Corbis; p.99 (BC): Juniors Bildarchiv BmbH/ Alamy; p.100 (T-1): Sally Anscombe/Getty Images; p.100 (T-2): DENIS-HUOT/ hemis.fr; p.100 (T-3): Ableimages/Getty Images; p.100 (T-4): Picture by Tambako the Jaguar/Getty Images; p.100 (T-5): David Muir/Getty Images; p.100 (T-6): Aldo Pavan/Getty Images; p.100 (T-7): GEN UMEKITA/Getty Images; p.100 (T-8): Larry Keller,Lititz Pa./Getty Images; p.100 (CL): Frank Krahmer/Getty Images; p.100 (CR): LeonP/Shutterstock; p.100 (BL): Dethan Punalur/Getty Images; p.100 (BR): Gallo Images – Heinrich van den Berg/Getty Images.

Commissioned photography by Gareth Boden: p.13 (BR), p.23 (BR), p.33 (BR), p.45 (BR), p.55 (BR), p.67 (BR), p.77 (BR), p.89 (BR), p.93 (B), p.99 (BR); Jon Barlow: p.7, p.19, p.21 (T), p.28, p.29 (B), p.31 (T), p.41, p.43 (T), p.51 (B), p.63 (B), p.65 (T), p.72 (T), p.75 (T), p.78 (C), p.78 (B), p.83 (T), p.85 (B), p.87 (T)

Our special thanks to the following for their kind help during location photography:

Radmore Farm Shop, Queen Emma primary School

Front Cover photo by **Premium/UIG/Getty Images**

Front Cover illustration by **Premium/UIG/Getty Images**